SOMETHING CLOUDY,
SOMETHING CLEAR

By TENNESSEE WILLIAMS

TENNESSEE WILLIAMS

SOMETHING CLOUDY, SOMETHING CLEAR

WITH AN INTRODUCTION BY
EVE ADAMSON

A NEW DIRECTIONS BOOK

Very special thanks are due to Thomas Keith, who worked with Eve Adamson to prepare a text of *Something Cloudy, Something Clear* that accurately reflects the play as performed by the Jean Cocteau Repertory.

Manufactured in the United States of America
New Directions Books are printed on acid-free paper.
First published clothbound in 1995
Published simultaneously in Canada by Penguin Books Canada Limited

Library of Congress Cataloging-in-Publication Data

Williams, Tennessee, 1911–1983.
    Something cloudy, something clear / Tennessee Williams ; with an introduction by Eve Adamson.
        p.   cm.
    ISBN 0–8112–1310–2
    1. Dramatists, American—20th century—Drama.   2. Young men—Massachusetts—Cape Cod—Drama.   I. Title.
PS3545.I5365S64   1995
812'.54—dc20   95–35011
                                                                              CIP

New Directions Books are published for James Laughlin
by New Directions Publishing Corporation,
80 Eighth Avenue, New York 10011

INTRODUCTION

I first met Tennessee Williams on Thanksgiving Day, 1978, on the stage of my theatre, Jean Cocteau Repertory. A German television company had rented the stage to film him reading excerpts from his prose.

"What do y'all do here?" he asked me.

I told him that we were a resident company performing the classics in rotating repertory and that, along with Shakespeare, Molière, and the like, we had performed two plays by Tennessee Williams: *Suddenly Last Summer* and *In the Bar of a Tokyo Hotel*.

"The *Tokyo Bar!* That's my favorite play and no one's ever really understood it. Please, please do it again," he said.

And so it began. I directed *In the Bar of a Tokyo Hotel* for the second time at the Cocteau in the spring of 1979. Tennessee loved the production. *Clothes for a Summer Hotel* was in the planning stage, and he was justifiably nervous. He hadn't had a critical success on Broadway since *Night of the Iguana* in 1961. He had, however, been constantly writing. In the years I knew and worked with him, the last years, hardly a day passed on which he didn't write.

Along with *Clothes*, Tennessee had been working on several other full-length projects, smaller in scope but fascinating. After seeing *In the Bar of a Tokyo Hotel*, and encouraged by Mitch Douglas (his agent from 1978 to 1981, who guided his projects during that time with intelligence and strong personal commitment), he asked me to direct the most experimental of these: *Kirche, Kutchen und Kinder: An Outrage for the Stage*. It played in repertory at the Cocteau during the 1979–80 season. During that time *Clothes for a Summer Hotel* opened and closed, in my opinion misunderstood by the press; and although collaboration on *Kirche* had been intense and rewarding, Tennessee was devastated by yet another Broadway failure. He was almost seventy. He had experienced phenomenal success during the first twenty years of his career. He had been toasted, feted, and hailed as the hope of American theatre. The plays from this period had become part of our collective psyche. The last twenty years, however, had in the eyes of critics and public alike been a long downhill slide to scorn, pity, and ridicule. Deeply, irrevocably hurt by this seeming public betrayal, he nonetheless kept writing and writing, daring to venture into the terrifying, absurd, and fiercely beautiful psychic realm that lies below the linear, logical notion of life that most of the rest of us cling to.

I knew this, and while I was often frustrated by Tennessee the man, I was constantly, deeply nourished and inspired by Tennessee the artist. So when, early in 1981, again through the benevolent guidance of Mitch Douglas, Tennessee and *Something Cloudy, Something Clear* arrived at my doorstep, I was prepared to commit myself and my theatre without qualification to this play, whatever it might be.

I was not prepared, though, for the surprise, delight, beauty, and depth of the play itself. *Kirche* had been a collage of lyricism and bawdry, its form created by juxtaposition of passages from the original script and Tennessee's constant re-writes. Here, on the other hand, was a play with a throughline, with an absorbing plot and strongly drawn characters.

The seemingly traditional structure (especially in the context of his other work of the period) was misleading, however. *Something Cloudy* is not of the genre he referred to as "my early pseudorealistic plays." Nor, although it examines the past and summons the spirits of those long dead, is it either a "memory play" *à la Vieux Carré* or a "ghost play," as he labeled *Clothes for a Summer Hotel*. Rather, it is a delicately woven tapestry of past and present, vulnerability and toughness, impetuous action and mature insight. It seeks a reconciliation between love and art, life and death, and—to use two phrases which recur in the play—exigencies of desperation and negotiation of terms. The cloudy and the clear.

The cloudy and clear of the title refer literally to the eyes of August, the central character. A cataract makes his left eye appear cloudy. (Tennessee had a cataract in his left eye and underwent several operations for it in the 1940s.) A photographic double exposure could also be described as cloudy and clear, and double exposure is the key metaphor of the play. Two times, two selves, two sensibilities exist simultaneously in August. But also, hovering around and permeating the entire dramatic poem, is the double exposure of Tennessee Williams: the artist and his art, the man and his theatrical persona, immediacy and retrospect, time stopped and time flowing.

August is most certainly the young Tennessee Williams of that historic Provincetown summer of 1940. But what gives the play its special depth is that he is also the mature artist of 1980, who does not just look back but coexists with the younger self inside him. Kip, the draft-dodging Canadian dancer, was a pivotal character in Tennessee's personal life, as were the "Fiddlers" and "Caroline Wales" (pseudonyms for Lawrence Langner and Armina Marshall of the Theatre Guild, which produced his first full-length play, *Battle of Angels*, and Miriam Hopkins, who starred in it). Ghosts from pre- and post-1940 appear to August under their real names: Hazel, Tennessee's childhood sweetheart; Frank Merlo, his longtime lover; and Tallulah Bankhead, the charismatic actress who personifies the turmoil of his life in the theatre.

Only one character is solely created for this play: Clare, the spirited young woman who, although like Kip doomed to an early death, shares with August his awareness of double exposure, of past and present merging:

CLARE: You have a strange voice.
AUGUST: Are you sure you hear it?
CLARE: It isn't as clear as it was, that summer.
AUGUST: Forty years ago, Clare.

Having created Clare in the present and placed her in his version of the past, Tennessee/August can share with her the compassion she had and he lacked in 1940. In her company he can look back with clarity and tenderness, with the clear eye and with the heart, both at "that long ago summer in the shack on the dunes" and at himself as artist.

Most of the major critics were predictably—and, I believe, unjustifiably—unkind to *Something Cloudy*. The prevailing complaint seemed to be that once again Tennessee had failed to write another *Glass Menagerie*, *Streetcar*, or *Cat on a Hot Tin Roof*. But why at age seventy should he have repeated what he had already done in his thirties? No real artist does. Picasso made line drawings and paper sculpture late in life, and no one demanded that he repeat *Guernica* or remain perennially in his Blue Period. It is a sad comment on our American culture that to the end of his life we censured the most original poet of our theatre for continuing to explore, whatever the cost or danger, the boundaries of his consciousness.

August tells us in *Something Cloudy:* "Life is all—it's just one time. It finally seems to all occur at one time." How generous it was of Tennessee Williams to share that last revelation with us.

—Eve Adamson

Something Cloudy, Something Clear was first performed August 24, 1981, at The Bouwerie Lane Theatre by the Jean Cocteau Repertory, New York, NY. It was directed by Eve Adamson; set and costume design were by Douglas McKeown; lighting design was by Giles Hogya; Kip's dance was choreographed by Richard Peck. The cast, in order of appearance, was as follows:

AUGUST	CRAIG SMITH
KIP	ELTON CORMIER
CLARE	DOMINIQUE CIERI
A MERCHANT SEAMAN	DAVID FULLER
MAURICE FIDDLER	JOHN SCHMERLING
CELESTE FIDDLER	PHYLLIS DEITSCHEL
CAROLINE WALES	MEG FISHER
BUGSY BRODSKY	HARRIS BERLINSKY

and the voices of J.D. EICHE, CORAL S. POTTER, JUDY JONES, and JERE JACOB

TIME: September, 1940 and September, 1980.

SET: A time and sun-bleached shack on dunes rolling upward like waves of pale sand-colored water, occasionally, sparsely, scattered with little clumps of light green beach grass. The large windows have no panes, the front and side walls are transparencies, and there is no door, just the frame. Part of the roof is missing. Adjoining this somehow poetic relic of a small summer beach house is a floor, a platform, all that remains of a probably identical beach house that was demolished more completely by a storm. Shimmering refractions of sunlight from the nearby sea play over this dreamlike setting.

The setting itself should suggest the spectral quality of a time and place from deep in the past: remembered, specifically, from a time forty years later.

PART ONE

At curtain-rise the front wall is transparent so that a wiry young man with a swimmer's build, his smooth skin tanned a shade or two darker than the dunes, is seated on a wooden box which serves as his chair when he is working. He is a still "unsuccessful" young writer. Another box in front of him supports a secondhand portable typewriter. He is completely motionless as though waiting for a signal of some kind to animate him and to begin the play. This signal is given after a few moments by the appearance of an apparitionally beautiful young man. The writer will be called August. The younger man is Kip.

At Kip's appearance the writer, August, snatches up some papers and a pair of glasses through which he regards the writing with distaste.

||||||||||||||||||||||||||||||||||||||||||||||||||||||||||||||||||||||||||||||||||||||||||||||||||||||||||||||||||||||||||||||||

AUGUST: Outline for—*shit!* [*He crumples it and tosses it fiercely away, drops his head in his cupped hands for a moment, then inserts a clean sheet of paper in the typewriter but does not profane it with a typed word for a considerable pause. Now on the dunes appears a young girl, Clare, also apparitionally lovely. She bears a wicker basket, and her long hair matches in color the refracted sunlight from the sea. Hearing her approach, Kip turns.*]

KIP: Hey, look at what I've discovered here!

CLARE: What?

KIP: Floor of some blown away beach shack and the floor's intact, it makes a perfect dancing platform. —How about that, Clare?

[*At this point August turns to look out at the pair on the dunes.*]

CLARE: You said you'd wait for me at the Atlantic House, Kip.

KIP: Did you get the note there?

CLARE: Yes, I got the note, just saying "I'm going out on the dunes near the lighthouse." This isn't near the lighthouse, Kip. I found you by your footprints. Lucky you've got such inimitable footprints.

KIP: You sound breathless, Clare.

CLARE: Yes, I—woke up that way—still am.

KIP: Sit down. [*She sits beside him, leaning against his shoulder.*] I don't like to go in the Atlantic House.

CLARE: Why?

KIP: —Oh—

CLARE: You receive too much attention there.

KIP: Shh!

[*August comes out of the shack and crosses to the platform as if he didn't see them, but he says "excuse me" as he throws himself on his belly and roots out from under the platform a portable phonograph, a wind-up victrola. Silence except for the sea's boom. He grins at them quickly and starts back toward the shack with the phonograph, then remembers another item and comes back to remove a rum bottle from under the platform. He then goes on back to the shack, sets up the victrola, then sits down in front of the typewriter, and immediately starts to write like a man possessed.*]

CLARE: Was that real? Did that really happen?

KIP: He spoke, he said "excuse me."

CLARE [*rising*]: Don't you remember him from last night? On the wharf?

2

KIP: The one that wandered in drunk and just sat down without invitation and stared at me so long and hard I thought, "He's going to arrest me" or—

CLARE: —Or?

KIP: You know.

CLARE: Attempt your seduction? As some of those fake artists do who ask you to "model" for them?

KIP: That's why I asked you to talk to him.

CLARE: Why did you want me to talk to him?

KIP: Summer's almost over. The wharf will be closed and, well, I know that your dear Bugsy is coming here to collect you today.

CLARE: I will not be collected like a piece of garbage.

KIP: We're more or less in the same boat, Clare.

CLARE: Which is?

KIP: Both of us have to be kept because we can't keep ourselves. You by Bugsy and me by someone, too.

CLARE: Me by Bugsy! No, oh, no, not again.

KIP: Perhaps some other—some alternative to it exists. Maybe one person could keep us both. We could be two kept for the price of one. We shouldn't be separated, not—not for a while . . .

CLARE: I'm expensive to keep. The insulin, the periodic hospital stays that get longer and—what a lovely clear day! Let's try to absorb this light and—face dark later. . . .

3

KIP: Okay, love, we'll do that, but first let's try to get the future— [*He stumbles slightly. She tries not to notice.*]

AUGUST [*in the shack*]: Whatever there was of that . . .

KIP [*draws a long, deep breath*]: —worked out, resolved somehow.

CLARE: Anything specific to help us resolve it?

KIP: Him in there, I don't think he's as poverty stricken as the shack suggests. Last night he showed us a clipping from *The Times* about a play of his being sold for a Broadway production.

CLARE: Kip, we know that everyone isn't a Bugsy, but I suspect that everyone does want something in return for something, at least I think a huge plurality of people do.

KIP: We've got things to offer in return. We can offer—

CLARE: Yes?

KIP: Sympathetic companionship, home cooking, attentions that are needed by a lonely, single person like—

CLARE: Him in there? [*Then lightly mocking:*] Young and not bad-looking. Are you enamored?

KIP: Clare, stay serious a while—then the jokes, huh?

CLARE: He looks somewhat unusual but—not queer.

KIP: I'd say he looks queerer than queer.

[*August inserts another sheet of paper in the portable. Clare looks through the window at him, seated in profile to them.*]

4

CLARE: You must've made that observation last night since there's been no chance today.

KIP: I noticed his left eye's a little cloudy but the other one's clear. There was something nice in the clear one.

CLARE: I get the impression, Kip, that you're putting him on a list of possible protectors.

KIP: I think that anything possible ought to be explored now. For about six months now you thought you knew something that I didn't. I did, just didn't admit it, like hoping a thing will go away if you don't look at it, Clare.

[*Pause: shimmering light, gulls' cries.*]

CLARE [*rising from the platform*]: Exencies of desperation . . .

KIP: The word is "exigencies."

CLARE: But desperation was right. Go on with your dancing, love, and I'll— [*There is the sound of wind and Clare covers her eyes.*] Sand! —I'll continue last night's conversation with this— possibility.

[*Throughout this duologue on the platform, it should be apparent that August is, indeed, listening to it with interest. Clare goes, now, to the window of the shack that faces the platform.*]

CLARE [*with a quick, light laugh*]: There's no pane of glass in the window.

[*August jerks the page from the typewriter and tears it up.*]

AUGUST: No. No, there isn't.

5

CLARE: May I . . . ? [*No response from August. She enters.*] Oh, I'm sorry. I'm interrupting your work.

AUGUST: You did me a favor by that. I was about to make a concession to the taste of someone else, a powerful man with practically no taste.

CLARE: Then why were you about to make the concession?

AUGUST: Because there are certain vital necessities such as money on which to survive.

CLARE: I think any kind of an artist—but never mind—my presumption—I'm—breathless—

AUGUST: You do seem breathless. Been running on the beach?

CLARE: No, no, just—an argument with my brother.

AUGUST: Breathtaking, is he? —Sit down.

CLARE: On what?

AUGUST: Chair or the—?

CLARE: That cot's a mess.

AUGUST: I'm a restless sleeper.

CLARE: I was about to offer a moral judgment of some kind.

AUGUST [*smoothing covers*]: On disorderly cots?

CLARE: No, not cots. Concessions in art, no less. [*She clears her throat.*] You resume your seat while I—

AUGUST: Pontificate?

CLARE: I think.

AUGUST: Do you? Are you sure that you're thinking?

CLARE [*with sudden urgency*]: *Not yet!*

AUGUST [*smiling, slowly*]: The double exposure. You're right. I concede that point.

KIP [*at the window, interrupting*]: Excuse me.

CLARE: What is it, Kip? Oh, Kip, this is—

KIP [*extending his hand through the window*]: Oh. Yes, we met last night. Do you have any drinking water in here?

AUGUST: A bottle of tepid soda.

KIP: Fine. Anything wet but not salty.

CLARE [*to Kip*]: I'm about to deliver a lecture to him on making concessions in art.

KIP: For or against?

CLARE: I think any kind of artist—a painter like Van Gogh, a dancer like Nijinsky—

AUGUST: Both of them went mad.

CLARE: But others didn't, refused to make concessions to bad taste and yet managed survival without losing their minds. That's purity. You've got to respect it or not.

AUGUST: I do, I will. But it will be years before I've mastered the craft of my work. I'll try to survive the time till then.

CLARE: You're young and strong and healthy. I don't know your talent, but if you do and it's good—forget concessions.

AUGUST: You have a rather precocious—knowledge of such things.

CLARE: Had to have that, exigency of—

AUGUST: —Survival?

CLARE: Had to have that early.

AUGUST: Why so early?

CLARE: My family in Newport, Rhode Island, were shocked by my lack of the conventions they valued too much.

KIP: Wow! I'll continue my exercises. [*He returns to the platform. Over the following he begins a series of slow, lyrical warm-up exercises which will blend gracefully, later, into the pavane.*]

CLARE: So—I learned to outwit them precociously, had no other option.

AUGUST: I'll make many mistakes but they'll be my own mistakes, I'll never concede to manipulation by—

CLARE: Don't—don't ever. In the end you'll take pride in having never.

AUGUST: We can delude ourselves, you know, now and then. Let's—drop this subject of why—

8

CLARE: Yes. A heavy subject. I just came in to ask you if it's all right to use your platform out there as a—

AUGUST: I don't own anything here but the typewriter and paper, and this little assortment of records for my silver victrola. I'm—just a squatter. [*He is pouring rum drinks into two glasses. Outside, the light lowers as Kip continues his slow, lyrical movements.*]

CLARE [*as August offers her the rum*]: None of that for me, August.

AUGUST: You know my name?

CLARE: You don't remember meeting me last night on the wharf?

AUGUST: You knew I did. But people seldom remember last night's names.

CLARE: What's my name?

AUGUST: Yours is Clare and your brother is Kip. Sure you won't have a drink?

CLARE: I can't. I have diabetes.

AUGUST: I thought only middle-aged people had diabetes.

CLARE: I'm sorry to say there's such a thing as congenital diabetes and I've got it.

AUGUST: I never heard of it, you look very healthy to me.

CLARE: Hmmm. —Doesn't it rain in, without any windowpanes or door to close?

9

AUGUST: Oh, sure. But I have this tarpaulin that I put over the cot, and I put my portable typewriter and silver victrola under the platform out there.

CLARE: You're a playwright. You told me that last night.

AUGUST: I write plays. Stories. Poems. Right now it's a play, yes. I was about to make a change in it that I didn't believe in when you called through the window, like my—like a—*conscience?*

CLARE: Don't you ever look at people directly when you talk to them?

AUGUST: Not unless I'm drunk.

CLARE: Why?

AUGUST: Why?

CLARE: Uh-hmm.

AUGUST: Because I'm getting a little walleyed and—a little dishonest, I guess.

CLARE: If you were dishonest, you wouldn't make such an honest confession of it.

AUGUST [*looking out*]: Beautiful dancer, your brother.

CLARE: You met him on the wharf last night, too.

AUGUST: I know, but—I was blind last night.

CLARE [*with an edge*]: Not too blind to stare at him like a bird dog at a—quail.

10

AUGUST [*turning to smile at her*]: No. No, not too blind for that. Well. He seemed oblivious to my attention, so I turned it on a much less attractive object, a drunk merchant sailor at the bar. He was a dog, in comparison, a mongrel dog. However. Beggars can't be very particular in their—choices, you know, and—beautiful as it is out here, it's also very lonely out here at night.

[*He goes to the victrola, places a record on it, and winds it up.*]

CLARE: You have a strange voice.

AUGUST: Are you sure you hear it?

[*We hear the record, Ravel's* Pavane pour une infante défunte.]

CLARE: It isn't as clear as it was, that summer.

AUGUST: Forty years ago, Clare.

CLARE [*closing her eyes for a moment*]: I feel—light-headed. Is it *déjà vu?*

AUGUST: You said not yet.

KIP [*from the platform*]: *Not yet!* [*He clasps his head.*]

AUGUST: Artists always continue a theme with variations. If lucky, several themes with numerous variations.

CLARE: But they musn't get tiresome.

AUGUST: Must take a chance on that as making concessions.

CLARE [*turning her head in sudden anguish*]: That, oh, I know that!

11

AUGUST: You should, you heard it often on my silver victrola that summer of—

CLARE: Please. Don't name the summer.

AUGUST: Life turned upon that summer.

CLARE [*fiercely derisive*]: Moth around a—

AUGUST [*indicating Kip through the window*]: *Flame!*

CLARE: *Stop!* Are you cruel? August?

AUGUST: I'd rather be cruel than sentimental, Clare.

CLARE: Nothing in between for you?

AUGUST: Yes, yes, naturally much. You know if you remember. [*He tenderly clasps her head between his hands a moment.*]

CLARE: Dead princesses don't remember their pavanes on your silver victrola. Is it as bad to die when you're young as Kip and I were and even you were that summer? Tell me. You've lived to discover an answer.

AUGUST: To live as long as forty years after that ecstasy. . . . It's enough to reconcile you to exile, at last, to the dark side of the moon or to the unfathomably dark hole in space.

CLARE: Perhaps you, perhaps he—

AUGUST: Perhaps I've transfigured him in my memory? [*He looks out the window at Kip.*] No. I've memorized him exactly as he was.

12

CLARE: This is the summer of 1940, August. Let's drop the metaphysics, play it straight, play it not like summer long past but as it was then.

AUGUST: Then! Yes! But I'm no prompter, you have to remember your lines. [*A pause.*]

CLARE [*as if awaking*]: —Why do you keep everything under the platform?

AUGUST: Under that floor of a next-door shack blown away.

CLARE: Why do you hide your valuables beneath it?

AUGUST: I don't always do that.

CLARE: Why do you *ever* do it?

AUGUST: Well, now and then, I have visitors out here.

CLARE: Thieves?

AUGUST: Potentially, yes. And what would I do if I lost my portable typewriter and my silver victrola?

CLARE: I see. Mmmmm. Did you hear our conversation out there? [*The sea booms. He grins without looking at her. She smiles slowly.*] My brother discovered that platform out there to dance on. I wouldn't have known he was here if I hadn't found his footprints in the dunes, pointing this way. He's very peculiar, my brother.

AUGUST: And very beautiful, too.

CLARE: Oh, that he is, too, he's that. If he wasn't my brother he'd drive me out of my mind.

13

AUGUST: He looks like the young Nijinsky.

CLARE: I'll tell him you said that. You see, Nijinsky's his god, his idol.

AUGUST: So he's reproduced the young Nijinsky for us. He has terrific control of his body. Is he a professional dancer?

CLARE: He's never danced professionally, but he's studied dancing.

AUGUST: You don't look like each other, there's no family resemblance.

CLARE: No.

AUGUST: You're both beautiful but in totally different ways.

CLARE: Oh, not totally, thank you.

AUGUST: Excuse me. I'm going back to work now. Without concessions, maybe.

CLARE: How long will you go on working?

AUGUST: Till I die of exhaustion. —But not now. [*Pause.*] No, a long time from now. Today I'd rather watch Kip dance.

CLARE: I dance, too.

AUGUST: I noticed that last night.

CLARE: I thought you just noticed Kip. When you stare at Kip like you stared at him last night, you're not seeing into his—

14

AUGUST: Mind? Spirit? Look, I work myself to the point of self-immolation before I go into P-town, and honestly, Clare, I don't go looking for rarefied minds or spirits.

CLARE: Have you got a toilet, I need to puke, I'm—

AUGUST: Ocean or dunes.

CLARE: Never mind. [*She sinks to her knees, head bowed. August kneels behind her, raising her head tenderly. Her eyes moisten with tears.*]

AUGUST: I knew you cared for him, Clare, very deeply, didn't want him used.

CLARE: I didn't want his body violated, to satisfy yours.

AUGUST: Clare, you have to know a person intimately, sometimes for a long time, to know about his mind, sometimes even slightly.

CLARE: I trust intuition about it. And in Kip's case, I had the advantage of knowing him in New York under special circumstances that—

[*They are both looking out the window at Kip. He had been performing slow dance exercises then he abruptly lost his balance and lowered himself awkwardly to the platform with a dazed look. Clare draws a startled breath. The music stops suddenly as Kip falls.*]

AUGUST: What happened?

CLARE: You offered me a drink.

AUGUST: You said you—

15

CLARE: I'd like a bit of it, now. Something happened to Kip on the platform, he—he stumbled.

AUGUST: Some of the boards on that platform sag a little. [*He hands her the drink.*]

CLARE: Thanks. Mind if I call him in?

AUGUST: No, I certainly don't.

CLARE [*at the window*]: Kip? Kip? [*Kip rises and approaches them looking a little vague but smiling.*] Kip, this is August, you remember him from last night. Doesn't he look distinguished?

AUGUST: It's awful to look distinguished this early in life.

CLARE: I think I meant marked for distinction.

AUGUST: As a—what? [*He is staring at Kip.*]

CLARE: Is something the matter, Kip. [*Kip seems to emerge from a fog.*] Excuse us August. Kip is terribly shy. [*She leads him back to the platform.*] I asked you what's the matter, love?

KIP: Nothing—much.

CLARE: Cut the bull. You're scared because you stumbled. That's nothing, nothing. I told you the boards on that platform wouldn't hold up.

KIP: I didn't just stumble on something, I—lost my balance and—things went blank for a—moment. . . .

CLARE: You're trying to make something of it, aren't you?

KIP: I think I'll take a dip now to clear my head.

16

CLARE: All right, but—careful! Stay in sight!

[*A nurse wheels the memory of Frank Merlo onto the upstage dune and leaves him there in the wheelchair. He is gasping.*]

FRANK: I'm worn out—had so many—visitors today.

AUGUST [*from the shack*]: Would you like me to go, Frank?

FRANK: They brought a priest, asked me if I wanted him to hear my—confession.

AUGUST: Confess! What is there for you to confess?

FRANK: It's regarded as a cardinal sin—you and me. To please them—sure—I said to him, Father, my sins are as white [*Coughs.*] as my blood is red. Why don't they bring my god-damned oxygen in? How long's it been since they wheeled me in here without any oxygen?

AUGUST: I'll call. [*He turns slightly in shack.*] *Nurse!* Mr. Merlo's oxygen! —He sat there gasping like a hooked fish for half an hour before they found time to bring his oxygen to the room in which they'd put him to die, inhuman sons of—

FRANK: Thanks. —Nurse.

AUGUST: He closed his eyes. Frank, are you sure you don't want me to go?

FRANK: No. I'm used to you.

AUGUST: For a man as proud as Frank Merlo, I guess that was a kind of declaration of love. But he turned away from me on the Memorial Hospital bed and pretended to sleep, so I— slipped out of the room to call a doctor. —"Christ, Doctor, he

17

knows, I know, we all know. All he's got left is his pride, don't let them break his pride, that he couldn't bear and neither could I! Do you understand me, Doctor?"

DOCTOR'S VOICE [*over the speaker*]: Yes, yes, August. There are circumstances when so-called medical ethics have to be violated for decency's sake. Now just let me give you something to calm you down this evening.

AUGUST: But there's tomorrow.

DOCTOR'S VOICE: Not always. There's a limit.

[*The inscrutable nurse wheels Frank off the upstage dune.*]

AUGUST: Is Frank all right, now?

CLARE: —Frank—?

AUGUST: Francesco Filipo Merlo! That was later. Much later. —Sorry, I meant to ask about Kip. . . .

CLARE: No, Kip's not quite all right. —Gone for a swim to clear his head. [*She sits down gravely. Pause: there's a shimmer of gold light over the dunes.*] I'm watching him from here in case he—

AUGUST: Isn't this a treasure to hold on to like dear life?

CLARE: Your silver victrola. I bet you've still got it in your head sometimes if not still in your heart.

AUGUST: I'm careful of beautiful things.

CLARE: I hope that also applies to people.

18

AUGUST [*cagily*]: Apply to? I don't understand. You mean am I—?

CLARE: As careful of beautiful people as you are of beautiful things.

[*Kip returns still looking somewhat dazed.*]

KIP: Clare?

CLARE: Yes?

KIP: Did Bugsy say he was coming for you tonight?

CLARE [*to August*]: I don't understand what he— [*To Kip with a look of warning:*] I didn't quite catch that. Whom were you referring to?

KIP: No one, nothing. Sorry. [*He walks away into the dunes.*]

AUGUST: Why did he—what did he mean?

CLARE: He goes into sudden lapses. Gets attacks of migraine and doesn't relate to the present.

AUGUST: I see. Migraine's a thing the medical profession's never quite explained.

CLARE: He doesn't relate to present, past or future when he—

AUGUST: You looked troubled, Clare.

CLARE: We're talking strangely, aren't we? I guess it's—

AUGUST: The loneliness of the nights. Sleeplessness on the dunes.

19

CLARE: I don't sleep well on the wharf. Kip's very good at relaxing massages, and the tide, sometimes, it laps right under the floor.

AUGUST: I just have my silver victrola when I'm alone.

CLARE: You speak of it so much, as if it had a special significance, like a—

AUGUST: Recurring allusion? It was the first thing I bought in New York when I came there on that sudden dispensation from the family Rockefeller, their foundation—gave me a grant. The silver victrola and the records I bought were reckless extravagance, cost almost half the monthly check but—I can't write without music—Bavarian blood in me. I'm one-quarter Hun. And the second thing I bought was a ten-dollar Panama hat, genuine, with a narrow black band. And the third thing I bought was a pair of good dark glasses, I mean from the drugstore, not from the five-and-dime. [*He puts on the dark glasses.*] These, you see. I'm looking right at you through them.

CLARE: I can't see your eyes now.

AUGUST: That's why I wear them, that's what they're for. The left eye, the pupil of it, is getting cloudy.

CLARE: The right one is perfectly clear and I find it very appealing.

AUGUST: Appealing for what? Sympathy? Forgiveness? [*He looks away.*] She would discover later that there was much to forgive.

[*A tall girl, with red-gold hair, face mostly obscured by a wind-blown, gauzy scarf, appears at the top of the upstage dune. She is a girl who was Hazel.*]

HAZEL [*calling softly*]: August? August?

AUGUST: *No, no, not now, Hazel! It's too late, Hazel. Not now!*

HAZEL: I knew. You could have told me and I could have told you that it didn't matter. August? —I loved girls.

AUGUST: You loved. You *loved!* That's all that matters, Hazel. I know that now. Remember when I couldn't face you directly, couldn't look into your eyes? A problem connected with—

HAZEL: Guilt over—

AUGUST: Secret dreams at night! With a penknife I bored a hole in the wall of a cubicle at the Lorelei swimming pool to watch—boys in the showers!

HAZEL: Oh, that. What of it?

AUGUST: Funny, ludicrous, that's all it seems to me now, but then—

HAZEL: I knew.

AUGUST: That I crouched at a hole bored in a cubicle in the boys' section of the Lorelei pool to watch the—naked boys shower?

HAZEL: Oh, August.

AUGUST: You said to me once, "Don't you know, August, I'd never say anything to embarrass or hurt you."

HAZEL: Did I ever?

21

AUGUST: No, Hazel. You never did.

[*Hazel moves slowly, haltingly off.*]

CLARE: Your victrola's run down.

[*August has dropped his head into his hands.*]

AUGUST: Has she gone?

CLARE: Who . . . ?

AUGUST: The sweetest and kindest, perhaps the one most loved—

CLARE: The girl you spoke of last night?

[*August is embarrassed. He takes a few hesitant steps away.*]

AUGUST: Did I?

CLARE [*breaking the silence*]: How old are you?

AUGUST: I'll be thirty next year.

CLARE: When next year, what month?

AUGUST: March.

CLARE: I love March.

AUGUST: Do you? I hate it.

CLARE: Because your birthday's in it?

AUGUST: Maybe. Yes. I guess. I hate getting any older, especially thirty. I once wrote a poem that went:

> *God give me death before thirty,*
> *Before my clean heart has grown dirty,*

CLARE: —Is that all of it?

AUGUST: No, it goes on. You want to hear more?

[*Clare nods, smiling sadly.*]

AUGUST [*squinting at the sky*]: Let's see. Hmmm. Oh!

> *God give me death before thirty,*
> *Before my clean heart has grown dirty,*
> *Soiled with—*

> [*He shakes his head with a wry grin.*]

> *Soiled with the dust of much living,*
> *More wanting and taking than giving . . .*

CLARE: That isn't all of it.

AUGUST: No, but this is no good, Clare, this has to be stopped. I wrote the goddamn poem at sixteen—of course it's absolute corn.

CLARE: Not corn for sixteen, sophisticated for—

AUGUST: Sixteen? Maybe I was sophisticated sixteen like fat ladies are stylish stouts or something. I was sophisticated and guilt ridden, devoted to a girl I'd loved since puberty. But she was precociously observant. Hazel loved me, though, she really did.

23

CLARE: You don't have to say it like it wasn't believable, August.

AUGUST: Being loved is a hard thing to believe and to love is—

CLARE: Hard to believe, too?

AUGUST [*looking out dreamily in the direction of the audience*]: All my life, at least since I started to shave, I've been like a kid on a grandstand, flag-draped, you know, waiting for a circus parade to come by. I hear the calliope in the distance. It gets louder slowly, that light, haunting music. But there's another sound, the sound of a thunderstorm approaching much more quickly. There's a sudden torrent of rain, a deluge— disperses all, all are dispersed except me. I stay on the deserted grandstand among drenched, motionless flags—always the obstinate waiter.

[*Kip has returned slowly from the dunes and is stopped by Clare. For a suspended moment they are frozen together listening to August.*]

KIP [*after a pause*]: How long did you wait for it, August?

AUGUST: I waited until a sort of faceless policeman in a black raincoat tapped my shoulder and said, "The parade's been rained out, son, it's been called off till later." But later still hasn't come. . . .

KIP: The black policeman was—

CLARE: —Death?

AUGUST: Sort of a likeness to it, yes. More a likeness to not yet being completely alive, I reckon.

KIP: Wind up the victrola, please. I think I've almost worked out the final movement of my dance.

AUGUST: The Pavane?

CLARE [*exchanging a tender, knowing look with Kip*]: Yes, the Pavane.

[*As August winds up the victrola, Kip drifts to the platform. Keeping her focus on Kip, Clare moves closer to August. The music begins. Kip dances in a cool light on the platform, August looking raptly out at him.*]

CLARE: I believe that you love, I believe that you love Kip, and I hope it's with the clear eye. What are you shaking for? What are you trying to cover up? I knew you loved Kip when you wandered in last night.

AUGUST: Last night I guess I sort of stared at him, huh?

CLARE: Yes! "Sort of"!

AUGUST: "Silent on a peak in Darien," yes!

CLARE: Stop talking gibberish, please!

AUGUST: Just a—literary allusion, a—phrase from Keats.

CLARE: We're not talking about Keats, we're talking about Kip and I want you to admit to me that you love him. Do that, admit that!

AUGUST: Okay. Quietly, Clare. —Certainly I love Kip.

CLARE: Louder. I didn't catch that whisper.

AUGUST: *Yes! Yes! Admitted.* —But it's downright madness.

25

CLARE: What is?

AUGUST: Me loving your brother who hardly knows I'm alive.

CLARE: If you mean that, well, your vision in both eyes is clouded over.

AUGUST: We're talking around something, aren't we? [*Clare nods.*] What are we talking around?

CLARE [*looking out at Kip, dancing*]: Kip's got to have someone keep him when he goes back to New York.

AUGUST: —Who? —Has he got anyone in mind for that?

CLARE: He has you in mind for that, August.

AUGUST: *Are you crazy!?*

CLARE: Shh, don't let him hear us.

AUGUST: What did you mean by that fantastic statement?

CLARE: —Well—

AUGUST: Hmm?

CLARE: You want to know all about him? Briefly?

AUGUST: Of course. Briefly or longly.

CLARE: He isn't really my brother.

AUGUST: Why did you tell me he was last night?

CLARE: I'm perfectly willing to correct the truth when it's for the protection of someone I care for deeply.

AUGUST [*grinning sadly*]: I see. I understand.

CLARE: Kip's a Canadian in the States illegally. He sneaked into the country to escape the draft because he has this passion for dancing, and he knew if he was drafted into the Canadian Army it would be too late, when he got out, if he got out alive, to learn to be a great dancer, which Kip is going to be, I mean he's going to be as great as Nijinsky. Well. He's in the States illegally. He could be stopped on the streets any time and asked for his draft card. That's why we stay off the streets nearly always. Oh, somebody gave him their draft card, but any time he might be stopped and not get by with that card and be sent back to Canada and not be drafted but thrown in jail for God knows how long, longer than he would even have to stay in the army if he hadn't skipped out of Canada before he was drafted. Are you following this? You're still staring at Kip.

AUGUST: Go on.

CLARE: All right, now that's one reason why Kip has got to be cared for, I mean kept, by someone, and it can't be me. I'm too young, I'm—a year younger than he is, I'm twenty, and I've got to finish my education, and—and—

AUGUST: Go on, go on, and what?

CLARE: I love Kip but I'm not *in* love with Kip. I was. Till I found out it wasn't possible.

AUGUST: Why wasn't it possible?

CLARE: Do you have to know that, too?

AUGUST: All you can tell me. Please.

CLARE: All right. [*She sighs.*] Well. I'm sexually precocious. You know how Alabama kids are. [*August laughs.*] Shh. —I mean I was doing it in the attic with my second cousin when I was twelve. We called it playing house. House in the attic. Awful?

AUGUST: No. Wonderful. But what's it got to do with Kip?

CLARE: Yes, you do want to know all about Kip. Well. He's lucky. —Maybe.

[*August shakes his head slightly, his face turning suddenly very grave. He rises and kicks a shell off the porch, for no reason.*]

CLARE: *Maybe!* —Well. —This part is embarassing. He'd hate me to tell this part but I have to because you've got to keep him. He's, well—

AUGUST: —What?

CLARE: Well, he's—impotent with me, and he—well, we— just share a bed together on the wharf this summer, for economy and because we like to be with each other, I mean we're like a brother and sister with each other with absolutely no incest, except I sometimes, well, I reach out to see if he wants me and he—well, he still doesn't want me. . . .

AUGUST: How do I fit into—?

CLARE: The picture? Christ, you're not a dumbo! Look! You're crawling around the frame of the picture. You've got to get off the frame, now, and into the picture. I mean you've been crawling around the frame of it and now you've got to get off the frame and hop right into the picture.

AUGUST: Hop? Into the picture?

28

CLARE: Yes.

AUGUST: How?

CLARE: Look, good God, you write plays. Just write a curtain to it. Can't you do that? Can't you?

AUGUST: —I—don't know, I—when I want something very badly, I—

CLARE: What?

AUGUST: —I start shaking all over.

CLARE: That's all right, do that, he'll understand that, August. [*She puts an arm about his crouched shoulders.*] Look, if you don't keep him with you in New York this fall, who will? Not me. I can't. I think your play will be a success, a hit as they call it. You'll have plenty of money coming in then, won't you? You can buy him dancing lessons; you can pay somebody to fake a better draft card for him. Can't you? Can't you?

AUGUST: This is a crazy, wild—dream. . . .

CLARE: Dreams are true, they're the truest things in the world, only dreams are the true things in the world, you know . . .

[*She has gotten to her feet, does an arabesque with her head thrown back and her eyes shut tight against the sun's glare.*]

I'll be in touch. I'll keep in touch with you boys. I'll—I'll fly to New York some weekends and for the Christmas holidays and so forth.

AUGUST: Wait! I want to ask you something.

CLARE: What? What do you want to ask me, I thought I told you everything you need to know?

AUGUST: No.

CLARE: No? What else!

AUGUST: How does he feel about me?

CLARE: Oh. —That.

AUGUST: Yeah. That. *Especially* that, honey. That's *pertinent*, you know.

CLARE: Well, we've talked it over, and he admits that he'd better live with you when we go back to New York since I can't anymore, since my family in Newport expect me back now, right now, and they won't send me another allowance check after this last one I got last night, special, after writing collect. God. Aren't families awful people?

AUGUST: What did Kip say about me?

CLARE: He likes you, he says, but he says he's afraid that he can't satisfy your, your—

AUGUST: My what?

CLARE: Your, well—your amatory—demands . . .

AUGUST: How does he know what they are? Hell, he knows I love him. When you love someone, you don't make *"amatory* demands." No. No. I'm being dishonest again. I would make amatory demands. I would want to sleep in the same bed with him and hold him all night in my arms while he slept.

CLARE: What if he didn't sleep? [*She laughs wildly, suddenly.*] He might not sleep! [*She picks up her straw bag.*] Bye bye, I've got to go to the bank to cash my check before it closes, bye bye! — See you later, Kip.

KIP: Wait!

AUGUST: *Wait!*

[*But she has skipped off, laughing. Kip stares after her, then takes a few shy steps toward August. Stops. There is still distance between them. He is self-conscious with August, and August is almost panicky near Kip.*]

KIP: What were you two talking about?

AUGUST: —You.

KIP: What did she say about me?

AUGUST: Too much. —Everything. —She shouldn't tell people you're a Canadian—draft dodger.

KIP: Oh. —I thought she'd told you that last night.

AUGUST: No. Just now. Is it true?

KIP: That I'm a Canadian draft dodger?

AUGUST: Oh, yeah, that and—Clare thinks—she said she thought that—

KIP [*drawing a deep breath before he speaks*]: I have no papers, the sort of papers you need to get any kind of employment. You know, any kind of—respectable, legitimate employment. Here. In the States. I—

31

AUGUST: Looking at his clear sea-colored eyes, I closed mine. It was as if I knew, even then, that I was in the company of someone immeasurably—

KIP: I have to walk about a little—and think. . . .

AUGUST: —*Doomed!* How goddamn stupid it is to look at them with envy, the perfect ones, the ones that appear to be completely, completely flawless, the—perfect—with eyes like startled flowers—

[*Loud sea wind.*]

—To walk and think about what? I think I know about what. The terms. The negotiation of terms.

[*Sea wind.*]

I'll give you this for that. A bargaining table. I wasn't prepared for it, then, didn't know how to shove my final chip on a single red or black square as the wheel began to spin. —The chances so wildly—unequal. One chance *for* you out of so many against. But in my blood was always, and, yes, still is—a willingness—I don't know how or why—to confront the almost-impossible-to-meet—challenge. —A chance? My last? —I'll take it.

[*Sea wind. Kip reappears over the dunes and slowly approaches August.*]

You've taken your walk and thought.

KIP: Yes.

AUGUST: Me, too. —I thought—I didn't use to know it was such a bargaining table!

32

KIP: But you know that, now?

AUGUST: As suddenly as if the sea wind blew it over me like this—storm of sand today. —What did *you* think as you—walked? [*Pause.*]

KIP [*with difficulty*]: I thought I'm forced to do now, the sort of things that don't demand—papers of citizenship—you know . . .

AUGUST: But do demand other things, not papers, but—other—things.

KIP: I—let's not talk about that. Huh? —I—don't want to talk about that.

AUGUST: —But, Kip, these other demands, you *do* submit to them, don't you.

KIP: Don't I have to? When I can't—you know—appeal to their better natures if they have them?

AUGUST: Do you think I have one?

KIP: —Yes. —I think I see it in the eye that's clear.

AUGUST: But even in the clear eye—surely you see *this?* [*He places his fingers on Kip's face.*]

KIP: Let's just talk, just—talk. I know how—involved this is.

AUGUST: Do you?

[*Kip nods slightly and gravely. A drunk merchant seaman staggers into sight and shouts:*]

33

SEAMAN: Hey! One Eye!

AUGUST: Jesus. He's coming back.

KIP: Who is he?

AUGUST: Merchant seaman I picked up last night, turned out to be sort of disgusting, puking and trying to make me do things I don't care to do.

[*He rises and confronts the Seaman.*]

Go away! Get away from here.

[*The Seaman laughs hoarsely and continues his wobbly advance.*]

SEAMAN: I hear yuh!

AUGUST: That's good. I meant you to hear me!

[*The Seaman still advances.*]

KIP: Let me handle it for you.

AUGUST: Just let him see you're with me.

[*Kip crosses to August.*]

SEAMAN: Got you another one, huh?

AUGUST: I'm with somebody decent, for a change.

SEAMAN: Hah!

[*The Seaman hurls an empty beer bottle at August but it shatters against the frame back wall of the shack. The Seaman grins viciously*

34

and comes on toward the shack. August starts toward him. Kip seizes August's arm and thrusts him back. He smiles at the Seaman.]

KIP: What do you want, what can I do for you?

SEAMAN: You queer, too?

KIP: No. Why don't you take a swim?

SEAMAN: Swim, I don't want a swim, I want a . . .

KIP: —What do you want?

SEAMAN: I want that goddamned fruit to give me some money.

AUGUST: If I give you some money will you go?

SEAMAN: How much money you got?

AUGUST: Enough.

SEAMAN: How much you think's enough?

AUGUST: Wait. I'll see what I've got. [*He enters the shack.*]

KIP: You don't want trouble, do you?

SEAMAN: I'm not scared of no trouble.

KIP: That's not what I said. I said you don't want trouble, do you?

SEAMAN: You ain't gonna give me no trouble, no motherlover gonna give me no trouble. I want five dollars out of that fruit, that's all, and I'll beat it out of him if I don't git it out of

35

him. I was here last night. He picked me up and brought me here last and night and done things to me like he wanted to make me queer, too.

KIP: You know that *you are queer*, don't you?

SEAMAN: Don't give me no trouble.

KIP: The truth isn't trouble.

SEAMAN [*stumbling—shiftily*]: —All you goddamn sons of—

AUGUST [*coming out of the shack*]: Here, Here. Five dollars. Now *go*, and don't ever come here again! Unless invited.

SEAMAN: —Lemme talk to you, buddy. Over there, over—here—

[*Clare comes running, panting onto the dunes.*]

CLARE [*to the Seaman*]: You come away from that house. You come back here with me. The beach taxi's coming. Come on, hurry, *hurry!*

[*The Seaman stumbles to her, stuffing the five dollar bill in his pocket. He puts an arm around her for support as they disappear together. Kip and August turn to glance at each other.*]

KIP [*smiling sadly*]: You see how things work out?

AUGUST: No. Watch them. See if she gets him into the beach taxi.

KIP: She will. —She has. She'll take him to the wharf and have the thing, the animal thing, I've not given her this summer.

AUGUST: What you said about your sister's not true any more than it's true she's your sister.

KIP: Halfway true.

AUGUST: No. No, not at all true.

[*The sound of a helicopter begins.*]

KIP: I meant—our relationship isn't a blood one, no, but—

AUGUST: It's—the helicopter's coming to deliver the local mail.

KIP: Mail? Delivered? Here?

[*The sound builds. They stand on the porch looking up at it. A sack of mail falls onto the platform and bursts open.*]

KIP: Gee.

AUGUST: Yes. Whiz. I hope it contains another option check for me. I gave my last five dollars to the son of a bitch that your sister rescued us from.

KIP: How much do they pay you? For your play?

AUGUST: They don't pay much. There's no formal option, not one approved by my agent or the Dramatists' Guild; it's a half-price arrangement, fifty a month, not the legally binding hundred. [*August is sorting through the mail.*] Of course that's an advantage to me in a way. I'm not so obligated.

KIP [*to himself, as though trying to work it out*]: Two people? New York? Fifty dollars?

AUGUST: They want the last act rewritten, but I won't write another word until they take out the regular hundred-dollar option. I have guts now. But I also had them then.

KIP: Now? Then?

AUGUST: Present and past, yes, a sort of double exposure.

KIP: I don't understand.

AUGUST: You're not supposed to, Kip. Here's a telegram for me! [*He rips it open.*] God. It's from them. They're coming here today.

KIP: Who?

AUGUST: My producers, the Fiddlers. And an actress they want for the play. If she'll play the part they'll take out a regular option. I don't have a watch. Do you?

KIP: In a hockshop.

AUGUST: I judge time by the sun. It must be after four—but then they'd make a point of arriving late. Oh, here they come.

[*The Fiddlers appear on the upstage dunes.*]

KIP: I'd better disappear until they're gone. I'll watch from the Lighthouse point.

AUGUST: I just have time for a dip to prepare myself for them.

[*They both race into the wings, furthest from the Fiddlers.*

38

[*The Fiddlers are a stoutish middle-aged man, Maurice, and his wife, Celeste. A world of opulence and fashion and of Medici illusions is apparent in them. Beneath this surface is an unfathomed depth of venality. In Maurice, the surface affability more successfully obscures the basic inhumanity, but in his tall, thin mate, you can almost hear the hiss of a venomous snake.*

[*There is the sound of the surf as they stand quite still for several moments, looking awesome in a Gothic way. Celeste slowly lifts an arm to shield her face with a gloved hand as the sea wind rises, lifting a cloud of sand.*]

MAURICE: She wanted me to see a film with Miriam Hopkins. I said, "Mrs., uh, Pardon." I call her Mrs. Pardon since I want to make it quite plain that her name's of no importance. "Mrs., uh, Pardon," I said, "Being a man of the theater, I don't go to the movies."

[*Celeste laughs with a vicious inflection.*]

And without batting an eye, she came back with this: "Mr.— uh—Fiddler, don't you want to know how the other half lives?" Then I topped her with, "I think you mean the other ninety-nine percent."

CELESTE: The woman's a real operator. You've got to be firm with her young client about your adamant refusal to negotiate with her or through her. Explain to him the nature of tenpercenters. That's what she is. And, please don't be taken in by his pretension of incorruptible commitment to his "art." We've heard it all before. He's just another male whore. I mean, imagine sending you that snapshot of himself in swim trunks. The implication being he thinks you're—

MAURICE: I'll thank him for it and say I've had it enlarged and hung up in my bedroom.

CELESTE: He'll believe it and price himself out of sight.

MAURICE: That shack must be where he stays.

CELESTE: Oh, yes, probably—to impress us with his pure child of nature spirit. Oh, Maurice, it's getting late, call him.

[*Maurice stalks down the dunes, calling "August, August!" Wind and sea sounds are heard again. Maurice cups his mouth and calls louder.*]

[*Now another woman, an actress, Caroline Wales, joins Celeste on top of the dune. She is beautiful, arrogant with pride.*]

CAROLINE [*loudly*]: The wind's too much, sand blowing in hair and eyes.

MAURICE: Let me know when it blows up your vagina!

CELESTE: Maurice! Don't be vulgar.

MAURICE: She loves it, don't you, dear? Don't you love it?

CAROLINE: Sometimes from someone but, sorry, not from you.

CELESTE: Oh, now, Caroline, you know Maurice loves to be outrageous.

CAROLINE: Oh, is that what Maurice loves. [*She comes down the dune.*]

[*Maurice shouts "August!" again.*]

CAROLINE: Oh, God, Maurice, you can't call August back in mid-September.

40

MAURICE: His name is August.

CAROLINE: I know, I know, but this *sand!*

CELESTE [*coming down the dunes*]: Darling, put your scarf over your head, here, let me do it, I'll fix it. [*She ties a chiffon scarf about the famous head.*]

CAROLINE: Thank you, but if he's not here?

MAURICE: There he is, getting out of the ocean. *August!*

CELESTE: Naked!

CAROLINE: Shall we pretend we don't see him?

CELESTE: He must think he's back at the "Y." That's where he stayed in New York.

CAROLINE: Now, Celeste, how can you expect a man that lives at the "Y" to write a play for me?

MAURICE: Playwrights are spawned in tenements and bordellos, then they graduate to the YMCA, then they graduate suddenly to Park Avenue apartments and grand hotels, and then they lose everything but their taste for booze and their outraged, outrageous egos, and finally, usually, they die in Bowery gutters from delirium tremens or an overdose of narcotics. We have to remember this cycle and make allowances for them. This boy has something, I think. We need fresh blood and he has it. Look at him running up here, like a— whippet . . .

CAROLINE: What do you want me to say about the play?

CELESTE: Just say if he makes the changes it might be possible for you.

41

CAROLINE: You talk to him about the changes, that's really not my department. I'm an actress. I'll look at him in speechless adoration. Struck dumb by his genius! He'll expect that, won't he?

CELESTE: You need a change of pace, my dear. The play might give you one, you know, it just might.

MAURICE: This boy's got something, it just needs bringing out.

CELESTE: What he's got is the biggest conceit of any pretentious young writer I've ever run into, and as for bringing it out, it's so far out it'll never go back in.

MAURICE: It isn't easy for a poet in the theater. Remember Gene, poor Gene. They say his hands are so shaky lately he can hardly sign a letter, and his wife says that it's—

[*The sea booms.*]

CELESTE: What's he doing now, Maurice? What's holding him up?

MAURICE: His towel fell off.

CELESTE: Just get the rewrites from him, if he's done any rewrites, and let's go on to Dennis. It's very late.

CAROLINE: Surely they'll hold the curtain for us since they know the Fiddlers are coming.

MAURICE [*shouting*]: We'd just about given you up!

AUGUST: Your telegram just arrived. [*He faces Caroline.*] Oh! Miss Wales! You! Does this mean you'll do my play?

42

CAROLINE: Well, it's quite a challenge—if you think I'd be worthy of it, Mr., uh—

MAURICE: This is our young genius. August, you remember Celeste?

AUGUST: Yes, of course. Mrs. Fiddler. I was so stunned at seeing Miss Wales here that—

CAROLINE: Sweet! Maurice tells me you're doing some revisions. Are you?

AUGUST: Yes.

CAROLINE: How are they coming?

AUGUST: I don't know. I hope so. Let's say, just say, I'm working hard as I can and—

[*The sea booms.*]

—my nerves are shot: it's chronic, they're always shot.

CELESTE: What's wrong with your nerves, August?

AUGUST: Constant hemorrhage.

CELESTE: Hemorrhage of the nerves? That's a new one.

MAURICE: He's speaking figuratively.

CELESTE: Oh. But there *are* some rewrites, August?

AUGUST: Yes, there are always rewrites, but how do I know they're what Mr. Fiddler wants?

43

CELESTE: August, Maurice sent you an outline for the last act.

AUGUST: Yes, but I—didn't read that.

MAURICE: *Didn't? Read it? Even?* Did you hear that? He didn't even read it.

AUGUST: No, you see, I have a new conception of the last act myself, and I wanted to try that first before I exposed myself to another influence, even from Mr. Fiddler—excuse me—I'll—uh, get—dressed. . . . [*He darts into the shack.*]

CELESTE: I think, considering what he just said, we might as well go and be on time for the show.

MAURICE: Not quite yet.

[*August returns carrying a bottle of rum.*]

CELESTE: Rum? Oh, yes, part of the sailor's tradition.

CAROLINE: I happen to love rum. May I try it? [*August pours her a drink.*] Mmm. Thank you. No sand in it, good.

AUGUST: Mrs. Fiddler.

CELESTE: We didn't drop by for cocktails, August. What's the time, now, Maurice? I can't see my watch through this veil and I can't take off the veil without being blinded by sand.

MAURICE: The wind's stopped now.

CELESTE: Momentarily, maybe. [*But she draws the chiffon scarf back from her face.*] It's already after five. It's a fifteen minute drive into town in the dune taxi, and from there it's three hours to Dennis which means we'd have to skip dinner to see the play at the Playhouse.

MAURICE: Celeste, if you're going to be a bitch, go back to the dune taxi with Caroline. I have to explain some things to this young genius.

AUGUST: Mrs. Fiddler, your husband, he mistakes irrational behavior and hysterical writing for genius, or at least he pretends to. But I don't want to hold you up. All I want to know is if you're buying my play or not, and if you really are, and will sign a regular contract with my agent, I'd like—well, I'd like a little cash in advance on the first option check, because, as I told you, my fellowship money is all gone now, I don't have any credit in town, all my friends are destitute or practically, my, uh, I spent my last bit of cash on a bottle of rum and—pineapple juice, one paper, glasses and . . .

[*The sea booms.*]

CAROLINE: Does it always blow like this?

AUGUST: What? No. It's the—what do they call it?—the autumn equinox starting . . .

CAROLINE: How long do you plan to stay on here, Mr., uh, August?

AUGUST: I have no plans, Miss Wales.

CAROLINE: What do you do about companionship with all this . . . desolation?

AUGUST: Nothing. Nothing much. Now and then I go into P-town and pick up somebody.

CAROLINE: Oh. A girl or a boy?

45

AUGUST: Miss Wales, if you'd ever lived in solitude on dunes, with such an impersonal companion as the Atlantic Ocean, you'd know that sometimes it doesn't matter if it's a girl or a boy.

[*Maurice chuckles. Celeste grimaces.*]

CAROLINE: I do understand. When a young couple has a girl baby they invariably say, "It doesn't matter to us if it's a boy or a girl," but you can see which they wanted.

CELESTE: August? We really do have to go. The rewrites?

AUGUST: I've done a good deal of work, but how do I know it will suit you?

CELESTE: I repeat that you have Maurice's outline.

AUGUST: Outlines don't work for me, Mrs. Fiddler. I don't want any ideas but my own right now.

CELESTE: August, you must face facts. Maurice can't give you another dime till you've done the rewrites demanded! *Caroline!* [*Celeste stalks upstage over the dunes, followed by Caroline, then stops.*]

AUGUST: My agent says not to give Maurice another scrap of paper till I have a regular Dramatists' Guild contract with him.

MAURICE: An artist shouldn't deal with agents and unions. I told you that this was a special arrangement just between you and me and you gave me your promise to keep it strictly that way.

AUGUST: Mr. Fiddler, Maurice, I have to live and I can't live without eating and my fellowship has run out.

CELESTE: The understanding as I remember it, August, was that you would deliver a complete second draft of the play by the first of September and it's now the fifteenth.

MAURICE: You know we don't want to take advantage of you, dear boy, but we have to stick to agreements, don't we? I'm an artist myself. I understand artists' problems. I'm famous for my sympathy with young writers.

AUGUST: I know, but you don't want to pay them, Mr. Fiddler—Maurice.

CELESTE: It's late, the sand's intolerable. This primitive life is an affectation that doesn't impress me, I'm sorry, Maurice, but—

MAURICE: Celeste? Remember how Gene lived in Province-town before we rescued him from it?

CELESTE: Yes. Drunk.

AUGUST: Was he? Perhaps I should emulate his—example. [*He drains his glass.*]

MAURICE: You'll learn as Gene did that drunkeness isn't indispensible to genius.

AUGUST: Shit, genius—excuse me, Miss Wales.

[*She laughs gaily.*]

CELESTE: You might beg my pardon, too. Scatological lan-guage is even less essential to genius, I'm afraid.

AUGUST: Mrs. Fiddler, your husband told me that I was a genius last month in New York. I know he was making fun of

47

me when he called me that but wouldn't sign a regular contract with me.

CELESTE: I smell blackmail here. Detestable extortion. Maurice, let's go before the dune taxi leaves us stranded with this—

AUGUST: This what? I'd like to know.

CELESTE: You'll find out the hard way. Caroline, let's go. — Maurice?

MAURICE: Yes, you girls go. Hold the taxi. I know how to talk to this boy. We have a rapport. Artists speak the same language.

AUGUST: Even with such a huge gulf between them as great wealth and—destitution?

MAURICE: A spiritual bond is what matters. August? You must learn to trust.

AUGUST: My agent advises the opposite, Mr.—Maurice.

MAURICE: Artists inhabit one world, agents another.

CELESTE [*from beyond the dunes*]: Maurice!

AUGUST: Your wife sounds seriously impatient.

MAURICE: We're expected in Dennis and Tallulah will not hold the curtain, never, you know southern ladies, autocratic as—*Coming!*—August, go fetch the rewrites.

AUGUST: When you take out your wallet, Mr.—Maurice.

48

[*Maurice pulls a roll of bills from his pocket.*]

MAURICE: Naturally I intended to relieve your difficulties. [*He peels off a bill.*]

AUGUST: That's just *half* a hundred.

MAURICE: You're a good businessman for an artist. Here's twenty more.

AUGUST: My agent insists that I get a hundred-a-month type of regular option money.

MAURICE: Never mind what that ten-percenter "insists." However—I do want you to live better, August, so— [*He peels more bills off his roll of currency.*] I believe this makes a full hundred.

AUGUST: Thanks, Maurice. I'll bring out the rewrites now.

MAURICE: Do that. Hurry. We're late.

[*August darts into the shack and then back out with a disorderly bunch of typed pages.*]

You young geniuses! —Are these pages numbered in sequence?

AUGUST: Yeah, yeah. Be careful with them, Maurice—I don't make carbons, you know.

CAROLINE [*returning from over the top of the dune*]: It's my turn to talk to him now. You all go hold the dune taxi.

MAURICE: Everything's fixed, we can go.

49

CAROLINE: Well, still, I'd like to talk to him first. I hope to get to know him rather well. August, may I talk to you for a minute?

[*Maurice goes up the dune arranging the pages.*]

—Well, now. What do you feel about Broadway?

AUGUST: I'd like to have a play on it.

CAROLINE: Obviously you will. [*She sits down beside him.*] — I'm playing a little game with them. Could you see that? I have already decided to do your play this season. In fact, I already know a speech from it, the one I like best. May I say it to you? Would you like to hear me say it?

AUGUST: Of course I would, I'd be thrilled.

CAROLINE: I'll make an effort. "There's something still wild in this country, this country used to be wild, the men and the women were wild and there was a wild sort of sweetness in their hearts for each other, but now it's sick with neon, it's broken out sick with neon like most other places . . . I'll wait outside in my car. It's the fastest thing on wheels in Two River County . . ."

AUGUST: —Yes. —Why did you pick out that speech, it isn't the best one?

CAROLINE: Oh, for me it was. I'm something wild in this country. *They* don't know it, the Fiddlers. But I know it. I know it.

[*The sea booms.*]

High, low jack, and the game! I'll do your play this season, Honey, even though it's always a long shot. Don't mind them. I play my game and they have to let me win.

[*The sea booms.*]

—Solitaire! —You. Me. —A couple of solitaries, lone wolves, fighting the pack . . . always in makeup, always in masquerade. But what does that matter? There's the game and we play it to win, but sometimes we even win if we lose. . . . The Fiddlers are fiddlers but we don't dance to their tune. We're artists. Desperate, but artists.

[*The sea booms again.*]

Hurry back to New York, Honey. I'll have it all fixed for you and we'll be ready to go like a pair of racehorses.

[*From offstate Celeste calls out "Caroline!"*]

Don't be too lonely tonight, spend it with somebody lovely. Goodbye. I mean *au revoir*. We'll make it together—we have to!

[*She crosses to the dunes, turns to blow him a kiss, and disappears. The dune taxi is heard driving off. August goes into the shack. Clare comes across the dunes with a kettle of clams and a sack of salad things.*]

MALE VOICE [*off*]: *Hey! Babe!*

CLARE [*turning slowly*]: Bugsy. Don't follow me here.

BUGSY: You wasn't at that rotten wharf.

CLARE: No. What do you want here, Bugsy? —I wrote you it was finished.

BUGSY: Shit.

51

CLARE: Didn't believe me, Bugsy?

BUGSY: A kid in your condition don't call the shots.

CLARE: I said it was finished between us and I meant it, no matter what condition you're talking about.

[*August comes out of the shack and approaches them bewildered.*]

August, this is Bugsy. Bugsy Brodsky.

[*Bugsy grins with a slight jerk of his head.*]

August is having a play on Broadway, Bugsy. It's being produced by the Artists Theater and Caroline Wales may be in it.

BUGSY: That tramp? I wouldn't let her in my place last time she come there.

AUGUST: Why?

BUGSY: Cause she's a noisy tramp that goes with a bunch of faggots. She's got one to light her cigarette, one to hold her up on the floor when she's tryin' to dance, one to tell her dirty jokes, one to scream with her, one to carry her pills and her Mary Janes, one to blow her nose for her, one to get her home when she's passing out, but none to screw her. But maybe she's got one to screw, I mean with a dildo.

CLARE: Bugsy, don't talk like that, she's a wonderful actress.

BUGSY: Hell, she's a faggots' moll.

CLARE: You don't know her, Bugsy.

BUGSY: I told you she come to my place East Side till I eighty-sixed her out of it because she gave it the wrong kind of

52

reputation. She give one of her faggots a ten dollar bill to tip the captain, and the faggot would give the captain one buck and pocket the rest. I don't need that kind of trade. I used to run a faggot bar in Miami. I know all about 'em, you can't tell me nothin' about 'em that I don't know already.

CLARE: You think you know all about everything.

BUGSY: I know all about some things and one of them is faggots.

CLARE: Another one is hired killers.

BUGSY: I know about them, too, and I prefer 'em to faggots. Faggots would kill their own mothers and fathers—they're a bunch of Lizzie Bordens—that's what they are and you know it.

[*August returns to the shack.*]

CLARE: Bugsy, will you shut up?

BUGSY: Get into a decent outfit and let's go.

CLARE: Where?

BUGSY: Your time's up here.

CLARE: Let me decide about that.

BUGSY: All right, decide about it: right now.

CLARE: I've decided about it. Get away from here, Bugsy.

BUGSY: You look terrible, Baby. I had you in good shape before you come here.

53

CLARE: I feel fine, the first time in three years.

BUGSY: Take a look at this. [*He hands her a folded sheet of paper.*]

CLARE: What is it?

BUGSY: The real report on you from your last trip to the hospital. Read it.

CLARE: No.

BUGSY: Want me to read it to you? You're living on half a kidney.

CLARE: We all live on half of something—some on less. You live on—do you know what you live on completely, Bugsy? You live on . . .

[*Bugsy knocks her down.*]

—All right. Now go away.

[*Bugsy shrugs and goes off. August comes out of the shack.*]

AUGUST: Clare!

CLARE [*staggering up*]: Did you hear it?

AUGUST [*he nods*]: Who is he?

CLARE: Heard of the Firefly Clubs?

[*August nods.*]

Well, I was a firefly till—Bugsy retired me for his personal, private use.

54

AUGUST: Jesus.

CLARE: Yes. Christ. —Well, now you know. What's become of Kip?

AUGUST: Swam up to the Lighthouse Point while I received some—professional visitors . . .

CLARE: Bad as mine?

AUGUST: —Probably—not quite . . . [*Pause.*]

CLARE: Wait for Kip. I'm going back to the wharf.

[*August nods without looking at her. The sky is fading. He sits down on the platform.*]

AUGUST: The evening grew deeper with dusk and—still I waited and waited. Finally I thought I would spend the night alone with the sea and my silver victrola. Well—there would be tomorrow. In those days I knew that there would be tomorrows. . . . I could only see the turning beam of the lighthouse. Thought maybe Kip could hear me if I shouted! *Kip! — Kip, hey, Kip!*

[*Not Kip, but the merchant Seaman responds, appearing on the upstage dune.*]

AUGUST [*quietly*]: *Christ . . .*

SEAMAN: Lost your boy?

AUGUST: Now what is it? What do you want this time?

SEAMAN: I'm not gonna beat you up.

55

AUGUST: No, you're too drunk.

[*He sits down on the platform, his back to the lurching approach of the Seaman. The Seaman sits beside August. After a few moments he says huskily:*]

SEAMAN: Las' night you wanted to fuck me.

AUGUST [*wearily*]: Yes. But you wanted to fuck *me* and I couldn't accommodate you that way, Spud.

SEAMAN: Tonight I'm too drunk to fuck you, kid.

AUGUST [*with a quick, harsh laugh*]: I wouldn't dream of disputing the matter with you, Spud.

[*Pause: the dusk deepens.*]

SEAMAN: So you can fuck me for another fin and a drink. — Okay? 'Sat a deal?

[*Pause.*]

AUGUST: Yes, I reckon—we've made a deal this time.

[*There is a sound of the surf.*]

DIM OUT

PART TWO

SCENE ONE

The set is the same as in Part One. An actress appears on the upstage dune, a scarf covering her face.

ACTRESS [*in a thunderously resonant voice*]: Where is he? What part of the garden?

[*August is dimly seen rising in the shack and crossing to the door.*]

No, no, I want him to repeat it to my face!

[*August steps off the porch to confront her.*]

There you are, you drunk little bastard! What was it you said I did to your goddamn play?

AUGUST [*quietly but clearly*]: I said that you pissed on my play.

ACTRESS: Come in my house and repeat that in the presence of witnesses. My lawyers will haul you to court for defamation of character, personal and professional. They'll sue you for every fucking cent you've begged, borrowed, or stolen, you gutter rat, you impertinent walleyed little—come in the house! Say it. Shout it! Well, no guts? Are you scared to?

AUGUST: No. We both have courage, but I'll not enter that leprosarium with you.

ACTRESS: Ho ho ho! Ho *ho!*

57

AUGUST: Are you playing Santa Claus now? Is it a better part for you than that of the desperate lady you travestied tonight?

ACTRESS: There's an extension phone. Bobby! No . . . Tony . . . no . . . Archie! Bring that extension phone. I can get him for defamation of character right here in the garden. Courage, have you? Then address my lawyers. Repeat the scurrilous charges you made against me to them.

AUGUST: No. No. But not because I'm afraid to!

[*Wind and sea sound.*]

ACTRESS: Tell me then why you won't speak it out to my friends and protectors.

AUGUST: I'm afraid you have none, just—sycophantic—attendants that use you without compunction. There's another reason that I won't enter the house and speak out.

ACTRESS: Name it! [*Pause.*]

AUGUST: I love you. I do, I love your fierce spirit and I will kneel at your feet.

ACTRESS: Kneel at my feet and I'll kick you in your nonexistent balls!

AUGUST: A lady wouldn't do that and you're a lady. A lady that's a tigress. What happened tonight is you gave those fat cat fags what they demanded of you. And so you pissed on the play, you performed a classic role in the style of a transvestite in a drag show. But—I love you. Now, you have to make a difficult decision. You want to close the play here or go up country with it? —Remember how you dared them to laugh at

58

the raging tiger in you, up there at City Center? They didn't accept the challenge! Afterwards, yes, I did kneel at your feet, I kissed your slipper and you didn't kick me with it.

ACTRESS: Naturally, not publicly in my dressing room. Filled with—

AUGUST: Flowers, yes, and your idolators, yes! —Did anyone know who you were? —*I* did. Later, later, I'd learn through old family letters that we were blood-kin. I was proud of that, Tallulah, and later, when you were in a breathing machine, at a Manhattan hospital, they'd say to you, "What do you want?" —You'd reply, "Bourbon. Codeine!" —The last request you'd make . . .

[*There are sea sounds. The actress bows her proud head slightly, then lifts it high and turns away.*]

ACTRESS: —Later, later, not much later, but later. Well, good night—lover. I'm going home. Yes, I'm going to take your play up country. You go sleep. Let Frankie drive you home to bed. Drive you home carefully—I love you . . . [*She descends from the upstage dune.*]

AUGUST [*looking up at the sky*]: Life is all—it's just one time. It finally seems to all occur at one time.

[*The scene dims out.*

[*It is the following evening. August is working by lamp light to a record on the silver victrola.*]

KIP: —August?

AUGUST [*springing up*]: —God! . . .

KIP: No, no, just a—draft dodger from Toronto.

59

AUGUST: Where'd you go last night?

KIP: I had a lot to think over and talk over with Clare.

AUGUST: I guess I understand, but—you might've—let me know. [*Pause.*] You know Clare received a visitor here on the dunes?

KIP: Bugsy, yes. She told me about it.

AUGUST: He knocked her down when she—

KIP: She told me all about it. When he knocked her down, did you see it?

AUGUST: —Naturally I saw it. I'd heard the shouting out here.

KIP: But didn't come out.

AUGUST: I came out before he knocked her down. I went back in. I came out again after.

KIP: Didn't stay with her.

AUGUST: Kip, I'm no contender for the heavyweight title in guts of the kind it takes to stand up against a killer like Brodsky.

KIP: No.

AUGUST: A faggot-hater, carrying a pistol. And I have work to live for. Will have for a long time yet.

KIP [*alluding to the record on the victrola*]: "Sweet Lelani."

AUGUST: Heavenly Flower, yeah. Not all my records are classics.

60

KIP: —Catholic tastes . . .

AUGUST: Hawaiian.

KIP: I know. I meant—

AUGUST: I know. [*Pause.*]

KIP: You didn't let Clare see your—attitude about her other life?

AUGUST: I didn't make any comment but she's a perceptive girl. And was a Firefly in one of his clubs till he took her as a mistress.

KIP: Look at her eyes, they're both clear as the sky.

AUGUST: Why'd she pretend she had a Newport background?

KIP: You rewrote the last act of your play to get it on Broadway with a Hollywood star.

AUGUST: Without compromising the inner truth of it, Kip.

KIP: Hmm. —When she comes back here—

AUGUST: Will she?

KIP: Oh, yes. If not tonight, tomorrow. Be kind to her, not patronizing.

AUGUST: But this professional killer, Bugsy Brodsky—

KIP: Some of us don't have choices, things are imposed— don't you understand?

AUGUST: That, yes.

KIP: You're shaking.

AUGUST: The nights are chilly out here, Kip. —Let's go in.

KIP: It wouldn't be any warmer in the shack.

AUGUST: I have covers on the—

KIP: Give me a little time.

AUGUST: Time, time, we all want more of that than there is of it to be had.

KIP: Let me wait alone a while. She might come back.

AUGUST: And the night will be hers? Again?

KIP: If she comes back, I don't think she'll stay. She—knows the exigencies of desperation.

AUGUST: Is that how you feel about it?

KIP: I don't know yet. Your victrola's run down.

AUGUST: Want to wind it up and pick out a record you like?

[*Kip goes into the shack.*]

I was happy. I was crazily happy. I thought maybe now the parade . . .

[*Kip has selected Villa-Lobos'* Bachiana's brasileiras No. 5 *sung by Bidu Sayao.*]

KIP: I was surprised to find this record in there.

62

AUGUST: You've noticed the catholicity of my tastes. I know the difference between old popular favorites and great music, Kip.

KIP: Which do you prefer?

AUGUST: Guess!

KIP: Music like this makes even tonight's sky clearer than it is. —I can only make out two constellations I know, Orion and Ursa Major. —So many visible that they lose themselves in each other. —I thought the falling stars, the meteors, were just in August.

AUGUST: Their schedule's not that strict.

KIP: Were you drunk last night.

AUGUST: Why do you ask that?

KIP: There's a sour odor in there and the floor's crusty with dried vomit. —Don't you mind it?

AUGUST: Preoccupied with work, no, not much.

KIP: What made you sick, was it me? My—not coming back?

AUGUST: I was sad that you didn't come back, I was hurt, but such things don't make me vomit. —I had a drunk visitor last night just after you'd slipped away. A visitor that vomited on the floor. [*Pause. The record stops. Then to Kip:*] How was Clare, how is she?

KIP: She's—she wants to be alone to think things out. She said I should go back to you and talk things out.

[*August laughs lightly.*]

Clare and I are the ones that are in the vulnerable position. You and Bugsy have power, not us.

AUGUST: I won't be put in the same category with Bugsy.

KIP: I knew you wouldn't.

AUGUST: Does Clare think I'm like Bugsy.

KIP: She wouldn't have dismissed me to your care if she did. You're shaking. [*Huskily:*] Would you like a massage?

AUGUST: Did you say massage?

KIP: Yes, in Toronto my father owned a bathhouse.

AUGUST: A straight one or . . .

KIP: I don't know.

AUGUST: Surely you could tell.

KIP: How?

AUGUST: Didn't some of the clients overrespond?

KIP: That's almost automatic, you know.

AUGUST: Didn't some of them whisper the number of their cubicles to you?

KIP: Sure, now and then.

AUGUST: Usually, I bet.

KIP: Oh, no, just sometimes. The place wasn't just for—the clientele was—

AUGUST: Mixed. But when you heard them whisper the cubicle number to you?

KIP: I laughed and said I was busy. And that was true. I'd discussed this with my dad and he said to always be polite but say you're busy and I was. —Didn't you say you suffer from insomnia some nights?

AUGUST: Yes, nights alone on the dunes when no one drops by to vomit on the floor, so to speak.

KIP: I'm a really good licensed masseur. I know how to relax you so you go right to sleep.

AUGUST [*laughs tensely*]: —No, no, baby, I don't want to receive an anesthetic massage. I'd much prefer to give a massage. Of course I'm not a licensed masseur and, frankly, wouldn't be trying to or apt to induce immediate sleep.

[*Kip is silent, expressionless.*]

Kip, we're negotiating for an advantage, aren't we? Like most people, if not all, sometimes? [*He moves closer to Kip.*] The air's, the wind's getting colder. Can we go in now?

KIP: The water's warmer than the air. Mind if I take a swim?

AUGUST: All the way to the lighthouse again?

KIP: Not all that way tonight. —Maybe I'll just take a little walk. It's late, I won't go far. [*He rises and starts off slowly.*]

65

AUGUST: His voice, it sounded almost panicky. Was I that terrifying, forty years ago? [*He calls out.*] Stay in sight. If you don't, I'll pursue you.

KIP: Call me if you can't see me and I'll call back. I just need to clear my head.

AUGUST: Why didn't you leave your clothes so I'd be certain of your return that time? —Following, pursuing would be a useless humiliation. I'll watch from here. [*He lights a cigarette, the match trembling in his fingers.*] —Headed for the water, the— artful dodger. [*He rises and calls out.*] *Kip!* —Again no answer, but he didn't swim long or far. Came back slowly as if approaching an "exigency of desperation," but with his clothes bundled under his arm. —Sound of parade came with him, unearthly calliope and heart beat fast. [*Kip reappears, glistening.*] I said something, not sure what. Oh. yes. [*To Kip:*] "Clare's not yet back, you see."

KIP: I really didn't expect her before tomorrow. Go on in if you think the shack is warmer.

AUGUST: Is your head clearer, Kip?

KIP: It is clear enough to think about things that we ought to discuss.

AUGUST: All right, let's discuss them, out here on the platform, Kip.

KIP: Last winter I knew how to go hungry in a cold, abandoned loft, south of the Village, on the Hudson River, and some of the windows had no glass in them, too.

AUGUST: No heat, no glass, no nothing?

KIP: I met Clare.

66

AUGUST: Where?

KIP: In one of those all-night diners a little uptown. I'd gone in not to eat but to apply for a job as dishwasher. She was at a counter eating chili. "Sit down," she said, "you're hungry." I said, "Sorry but I couldn't pay for food." She smiled and said, "Never mind. Order something, anything you—" I sat down by her but didn't order. "Eggs with bacon or sausage or—how about corn beef hash with an egg on it, you look hungry as hell!" —I told her, I knew I could tell her, "After three days, you don't feel hunger much." —She ordered me a Delmonico steak with french fries. —It's hard to get food down when your stomach's shrunk from such a long fast. I vomited, suddenly, on the floor, like your visitor last night. But I drank a lot of water and kept that down.

AUGUST: No water in the loft either? —Are you telling me a tall tale, Kip? —People will always give you water.

KIP: I did go out for water after dark. Till I met Clare, I was scared to go out, but I'd fill an old coffee tin with water after dark. —I would've learned how to die rather than kill, that's true, that's no tall tale.

AUGUST: —Have you thought of anything else we ought to discuss tonight, Kip?

KIP: Of course I noticed you look at me the other night. I asked Clare to talk to you.

AUGUST: Yes, we talked, mostly about you.

KIP: I know, she told me. She said you said that I looked—

AUGUST: Being drunk that night I'm not sure what I said. Oh. I think it was "saintly"—

67

[*Pause. Kip drops his head into his hands. After a bit he begins to sob softly. August draws close to him and puts an arm about his shoulders.*]

KIP: —I don't know where I am.

AUGUST: What?

KIP: What's happening? [*He rises unsteadily.*] I must've been in the water, I'm wet. —Have you got a clean towel.

AUGUST: I still thought it was possible, then, that he was giving a performance, and it made me say harsh things. I said, "Yes, I've got a clean towel in the sack, the shack, not one of those towels called joy rags!"

KIP: —Joy? Rags?

AUGUST: You know what I mean or you don't. [*He rises abruptly.*] I'm not going to explain. I'm going in and try to get that dry vomit off the floor.

[*August enters the shack and dampens some rags with half a bottle of soda and kneels to scrub the floor hard. When finished he tosses the rags out the door. He then goes to the window facing the platform and calls out.*]

Kip?

KIP: Yes.

AUGUST: Why don't you come in for the clean towel, or—

KIP: Or what?

AUGUST: Go away and look for Clare again, Kip.

68

KIP: —There's things that I don't know and things that you don't know. Such as—where do the—seagulls—sleep at night?

AUGUST: Never asked them about that.

KIP: You've lost patience with me?

AUGUST: I will if you stay out there with your "exigencies of desperation," Kip.

KIP: I'll be in, I'm just—

AUGUST: What're you doing out there?

KIP: Watching another meteor, a meteor falling into the ocean, way, way, off. [*Pause.*] —Gone, now. —I'm coming in. [*He slowly enters the shack.*]

AUGUST: Here's your towel. Not immaculate, but—

KIP [*drying himself with the towel*]: Don't be so angry with me.

AUGUST: I'm not that.

KIP: —I'm—dried off now.

AUGUST: Then?

KIP: —Put the "Pavane" back on the victrola.

AUGUST: Yes—music. [*He winds the phonograph and starts the "Pavane."*] Still afraid? Of love?

KIP: Not of love, but—

AUGUST: What?

69

KIP: —The—other. —Please. I don't know what to do.

AUGUST: Will you accept my instruction? [*Kip stares at him a moment, then slowly lowers his face. August waits, then takes Kip's hand.*] —He could have easily broken away, but he didn't . . .

BLACKOUT

SCENE TWO

The next evening. Clare appears on the upstage dune.

CLARE: Hey. Help me carry this stuff. [*August starts toward her.*] Both of you, Kip, you, too! [*Kip doesn't move.*] *Kiiip!?*

AUGUST [*as he goes to her*]: I can do it. Kip doesn't feel well today.

CLARE: What's the matter with him? Pick up the stuff back there. —Kip, what's the matter with you?

[*Kip doesn't seem to hear her. The sea booms. August follows her, laden with bleached branches in tortured shapes. Still ignoring her, Kip stretches out on the platform, arms folded over his face.*]

AUGUST: I don't think he slept last night.

CLARE: I wonder why.

AUGUST: I'll tell you about it later.

CLARE: Tell me now, not later. Did you break our agreement?

AUGUST: We—came to—terms.

CLARE: I don't believe you. He wouldn't unless you . . . —Did you?

AUGUST: The parade went by, it marched right by me, right by where I was waiting.

CLARE: He looks like it marched across him.

71

AUGUST: No, he's just tired this evening, let him rest a while, huh?

CLARE: Not yet, I have to talk to him. [*She crosses out to the platform.*] Kip?

KIP [*blankly, after a moment*]: —Hello, Clare.

CLARE: What's the—?

KIP: —Later. Alone.

CLARE [*going back to August*]: What's wrong with Kip, what's happened? He looks like a whipped dog.

AUGUST: Clare, don't you think Kip puts on an act sometimes?

CLARE: Anyone does, when forced to—if he can. What did happen between you since I saw him last?

AUGUST: We had a long discussion of terms. It was a— negotiating table out here, the same as it was between me and the Fiddlers and between you and Bugsy Brodsky.

CLARE: I got knocked down. Did Kip?

AUGUST [*impatiently*]: Did you see any bruises on him?

CLARE: The look in his eyes was a bruised one.

AUGUST: He's just very sleepy, that's all. [*She kicks sand at him fiercely.*] I didn't know fireflies could kick.

CLARE: Fireflies can be savage as you. I don't think you're a one-quarter Hun, I think that you're a complete one.

AUGUST: Just the great grandson of a Bavarian burgher, who came to the States to avoid army service, the reason Kip migrated from Toronto.

CLARE: Go swim, go drown, I hope a shark eats you.

AUGUST: Not so loud, let him rest. [*He goes into the shack.*]

CLARE: Kip? Are you all right or—?

KIP: I'm all right. I'm all right. I lived through it, like you did being a Firefly for Bugsy.

CLARE: He broke the agreement?

KIP: There wasn't a settled agreement, just—negotiation of terms, he called it.

CLARE: Let's go.

KIP: Where?

CLARE: Away.

KIP: Away to where? We're checked out at the wharf.

CLARE: I can check into the hospital again, and demand that you stay with me. Bugsy would pay, he'd have to, I have so much on him.

KIP: Bugsy would pay to have us both wiped out. [*Pause— gently:*] It's clearing up, it's going to be a clear night with many stars for fireflies . . .

CLARE: You sound resigned.

KIP: Clare, it's narrowed down to one last option for us.

73

CLARE: Him?

[*The sound of a helicopter fades in. It drops a mailsack on the platform, and the sound fades out.*]

KIP: Not much mail anymore in the sack.

CLARE: It broke open, and will you look what spilled out?

KIP: A telegram?

CLARE: To him, called the one last option. Tell me about it, for God's sake.

KIP: He had what he thought he wanted, but I don't think it was.

CLARE: Can you make that clearer?

KIP: He used me like a— [*The sea booms.*]

CLARE: Quick, let's get away quick.

KIP: Let's go through with the picnic.

CLARE: Why should we bother with the son of a bitch?

KIP: He isn't that, exactly. He's just—I think he's just about as desperate as we are.

CLARE: Make sense. We're—I'm going to die this year.

KIP: Is he the kind of person we want to hurt?

CLARE: All right, be noble, I'm going.

KIP: It's really clearing up now. Let's go through with the picnic. This is our last day here.

CLARE: Why are you rubbing your head.

KIP: You know why. It's come back. I knew it would and it has! —You brought some stuff for a salad?

CLARE: Yes . . .

KIP: I will—mix—the salad and—heat the chowder. Perhaps if I convince him of my domestic skills, he could value me for that. [*He enters the shack.*] I'm going to prepare supper.

AUGUST: Anything I can do?

KIP: Yes. Go sit with Clare, she's—depressed.

[*August kisses the back of Kip's neck, then goes to Clare.*]

CLARE: Yes, I know, he told me. What did you see in his eyes?

AUGUST: —I—couldn't see his eyes.

CLARE: That's what I figured. Come over here. Just listen carefully. I have to talk quickly and quietly. Don't answer. Don't say anything now or later. It's this. You've noticed how short his hair is, just barely long enough to cover the scar on his head where a piece of his skull was removed last fall at the Polyclinic Hospital in New York.

AUGUST: But—

CLARE: I said just listen.

AUGUST: How could he be a draft dodger if—

CLARE: He'd been in the States illegally for two months when this thing came on him with sudden blinding headaches. They told him it was benign, assured him it was benign.

AUGUST: It wasn't?

CLARE: No, it was a something blastoma. The most malignant of all. They let me know the truth when they found out we were planning to live together when—released. I think today for the first time he's guessed the truth. He just said now, "It's come back, I knew it would and it has."

AUGUST: *Christ.*

CLARE: Shhh. We've kept up, I've kept up the pretense and luckily until today there was nothing, almost nothing, just occasional little slight lapses of concentration that I'd laugh at or ignore.

[*Pause. Kip has finished the salad. He stands immobile, head lowered.*]

Of course there's no danger, now, that Kip could be drafted but he'd be taken back to Canada and he's all I've got in my heart, my life.

AUGUST: —Couldn't we all live together? For a while?

CLARE: Yes, but purely, cleanly. I'll not have you use him again like a whore.

AUGUST: I love him. You know I love him. —Would you permit me to hold him?

CLARE: The cloudy eye demands something, even now?

76

AUGUST: I think he'd want to be held, to be caressed?

CLARE: If that—would suffice.

[*Kip moves uncertainly toward them. August springs up.*]

KIP: Never mind. Go on talking to Clare. She's probably got more to talk over with you.

AUGUST: We were just planning to all live together when we got back to New York.

KIP: Good. Perfect. Go on making plans for that, August, while I—pour the chowder . . .

[*August turns back to Clare who is holding a telegram.*]

CLARE: You haven't opened this.

AUGUST: I'm scared of telegrams.

CLARE [*opening it and reading it gravely*]: You needn't have been frightened of this one, August. It's from your producers.

AUGUST: Fiddlers?

CLARE: "Caroline adores revised script. All set. Rehearsals beginning Friday. Get here Tuesday at latest. All send love. Hosannah in the highest. Waiting for you impatiently, dear boy. Maurice Fiddler."

[*Kip comes over with the kettle of chowder.*]

AUGUST [*quietly, in an awed voice*]: Life. —It's a lovely, clear evening.

77

CLARE: Yes, it couldn't be clearer. I'll go and help Kip. [*She goes to Kip who spoons out a taste of the chowder, blows on the spoon, tastes it, and says "Good."*] Yeah. Wonderful. Perfect.

AUGUST: How's the chowder?

KIP: Wonderful. Perfect.

CLARE: Well, it's—

KIP: —I think he must be an artist with all that intensity in him.

AUGUST: What?

KIP: Nothing.

AUGUST: I thought you said something about me being a one-eyed artist.

KIP: You're having auditory—hallucinations, August. Shall I rub the salad bowl with garlic?

AUGUST: Why not? We're not going to play post office.

CLARE: Poor August. He's disillusioned . . .

KIP: He never had the top of his head sawed off and an ounce of diseased brain matter removed from his top-piece, and he never had to choose between a charity ward and sleeping with Bugsy Brodsky. He never sat next to us for six weeks in that goddamn—show—blow—varium in— [*He rubs his forehead, confused.*] —Rose—shose—*pose! —POSE!*—for—faggot fake painters in— [*He stumbles and Clare catches him.*]

CLARE: August. Go have a swim.

78

AUGUST: I've had two swims today.

CLARE: Have three. Everything will be fixed when you come back.

AUGUST: *Will* it?

CLARE: *Yes, it will, go swim!* [*August picks up a towel and goes off. The sea booms long but not loud. Clare sits beside Kip.*] —I know what you're thinking, baby.

KIP: All that work this summer.

CLARE: We've all worked hard this summer, all three of us, and none of us, not one of us, knows what for, what will come of it.

KIP: The—choreographic—note system . . .

CLARE: You were fine today.

KIP: How do I know?

CLARE: I know.

KIP: I love you, Clare.

CLARE: I wasn't lying when I told August that we were brother and sister.

KIP: What are you going to do?

CLARE: Look. [*She presses her ankle hard with her thumb and forefinger.*] See?

KIP: What?

CLARE: This . . . Where I squeezed my ankle. See? It's still white where I squeezed it and I didn't squeeze hard. Fluid's started gathering in me again. In spite of the—goddamn Diural tablets, it's started to accumulate in my ankles again, then it will be in my legs, then it will be—

KIP: Let's go home.

CLARE: Where's home? Some hospital?

KIP: No, your room, our—room on the wharf.

CLARE: Yes, let's leave him his chowder and salad and one place at the table.

KIP: I don't want to hurt him, Clare. He's coming back.

[*August is returning from the water.*]

What are we going to do?

CLARE: You're talking all right, now. You know, I think it was just a panic thing.

KIP: So's your ankle, Ducks.

CLARE: Let's play it like we were a couple of massa-type niggers, wait on him, serve him like a pair of—

[*A loud boom of the tide drowns out her speech. Kip nods, with a twisted grin. He motions her to take the chowder.*]

CLARE: May we serve you, Sir?

AUGUST: Yes, let's eat, I'm famished.

CLARE: Yes, Sir.

KIP: Salad with chowder or after?

AUGUST: Put it all on the table.

KIP: Yes, Sir, as you wish, Sir.

AUGUST: It's a—beautiful evening.

CLARE: Yes, Sir.

AUGUST: Cut the crap, Miss Firefly. Sit down.

CLARE: Not until you're served, Sir.

AUGUST: I said "Cut the crap."

CLARE: A *firefly?* At the *table?* You must be joking.

AUGUST [*tenderly*]: You're the queen of the fireflies.

CLARE: Appointed by Bugsy Brodsky.

AUGUST: No, by me. This is my Firefly Club. I name you Queen of the Fireflies.

[*She glances at him for a tense moment, then drops her face, sobbing, into her hands. Kip comes over with the salad.*]

—Oh. The wine . . .

[*He crosses to the platform and digs a wine bottle out of the sand under it. Clare and Kip stand facing each other.*]

CLARE: Shall we take our plates inside? Servants eat in the kitchen.

KIP: No. That game didn't go. Mean games never go.

CLARE: Okay, you deal, you name the game.

KIP: Sit down and shut up. Let him talk. I want to hear what he says, now.

AUGUST [*returning with the wine bottle*]: Dune temperature: cool enough. —What'll we open it with? I don't have— [*He looks helplessly from one to the other. Then he sits down between them and drops his face into his hands. The sea booms.*]

CLARE: Kip, hand him a knife.

[*Kip picks up a knife. His movements betray a disequilibrium. August snatches the knife from him, drives it hard into the cork of the bottle, and works it savagely, prying the cork up a bit.*]

—Just push the cork into the bottle.

AUGUST: No, I'm— [*He seizes the cork between his teeth and twists the bottle. Clare looks at Kip who smiles at her, wryly.*] —Now it's out.

CLARE: The cork is out of the bottle, the cat is out of the bag.

KIP: Shut up, Clare. How's the salad?

CLARE: You try it, you made it.

KIP: Oh. [*He tastes it.*] I forgot the garlic.

CLARE: So we could all kiss each other?

KIP: Clare—Clare?

CLARE: If everybody eats garlic, then it doesn't offend—I mean each other. But my breath problem is different, it comes from—

KIP: You don't have any.

CLARE: Breath problem? Yes, I do. Bugsy says my breath turns sour when my kidneys quit on me. So he quit kissing, just—fucked . . . or made me— [*She covers her mouth.*]

KIP: Stop it, will you, please, Clare? This is our last evening together.

CLARE: The cat's all out of the bag.

KIP: What of it, what good is a cat in a bag? A cat's a natural wide-open night prowler, by nature, by, by—natural—way—nay—chure . . .

[*August turns slightly to look at Kip.*]

CLARE: Rub the garlic on the butt-end of the bread. Cut off the butt-end of the loaf and rub it hard with garlic and stir it around in the salad. Nobody's going to kiss anybody tonight with or without the comparatively, relatively sweet smell of the strong onion, the Hun of the onions. Where's the bread.

KIP: Here.

CLARE: Where's the knife?

KIP: Here.

CLARE: All right. The French call it a—Oh, God, what do they call it? They call it a *jabon?* No. —Well, never mind what they call it. They rub the dry butt-end of the bread loaf around the salad bowl and mix it into the salad and it—

83

[*August suddenly springs up and kisses her again and again on the mouth. Kip smiles to himself. The sea booms again and again but not too loudly.*]

—Well? Smell?

AUGUST: You have a mouth full of flowers.

CLARE: Goddamn half-ass liar.

AUGUST: Kip?

[*Kip crosses to her, kisses her sweetly and delicately, then draws back, smiling.*]

CLARE: Well?

KIP: Sweeter than roses . . . August?

AUGUST: Huh?

KIP: Tell her.

AUGUST: What?

KIP: How beautiful she is, the Queen of the Fireflies. It's dark now, it's time for her to shine.

AUGUST: When did she ever stop shining? Like the sky on the sea?

[*Pause. Kip rubs his forehead. August leans forward and places his fingers tenderly on Kip's face and along his wide throat.*]

Child of God—you—don't exist anymore.

CLARE: He might've heard you say that.

[*August shakes his head with a sad slight smile.*]

August, you know I have a suspicion that these little bits of romantic excess are going to get you into professional trouble someday.

AUGUST: Oh, that they've done already. [*He scribbles a note.*]

CLARE: What are you writing? What was that you just wrote?

AUGUST: Just a note of reference for tomorrow.

CLARE: A secret note for reference tomorrow. And Kip's already saying good-bye to this summer.

[*Music. Kip's finger performs a slow trajectory of a falling star.*]

AUGUST: That long ago summer in the shack on the dunes.

CLARE: I'll leave you to that secret reference for tomorrow.

AUGUST: See how light the sky is? Light as clear water with just a drop or two of ink in it. Note to end on? How did it go, that bit of Rilke? "The inscrutable Spinx? Poising forever—the human equation—against the age and magnitude of a universe of—stars . . ." The lovely ones, youthfully departed long ago. But look [*He points.*] very clearly here, and while this memory lives, the lovely ones remain here, undisfigured, uncorrupted by the years that have removed me from their summer.